Aldeburgh 2015

Gallery Books
Editor Peter Fallon
THE ROOMS

Peter Sirr

THE ROOMS

Gallery Books

The Rooms
is first published
simultaneously in paperback
and in a clothbound edition
on 30 October 2014.

The Gallery Press
Loughcrew
Oldcastle
County Meath
Ireland

www.gallerypress.com

ISBN 978 1 85235 603 3 *paperback*
     978 1 85235 604 0 *clothbound*

A CIP catalogue record for this book
is available from the British Library.

The Rooms receives financial assistance
from the Arts Council.

Contents

for Enda and Freya

The Mapmaker's Song

The mapmaker downed his tools.
I've caught it: every alley, every street,
every fanlight and window ledge,
the city fixed and framed.

Now I want everything else.
I want to be a historian of footsteps,
a cartographer of hemlines and eyelids,
I want to catch what the pavements say

when they sing to each other
in their deep laboratories, plotting
every journey since the place began.
I want the whole

unlosable database, the repeating place,
kings stalking the server farms,
tailbacks and looped alarms,
I want to be where

brushstrokes flicker on a bank of screens,
where graveyards tilt
and quiet populations crowd the air,
their quarters risen again,

their furniture
smashing through the floors.
I want to stand at the centre
of a great clutter

mapping ashes, mapping bones:
archivist, enumerator, hanger-on
signing the returns
of an infinite census.

I want to be,
beyond everything I've reached or drawn,
not much at all, or all there is,
a geographer of breath

a curator of hands.
I want to lie in the atrium
of the museum of the fingertip
and touch, touch, touch.

Sold

Imagine staying still,
rooted to the spot,
to the five-hundred-year-old
brick floor of a house
in a quiet valley, listening
to the bricks — *I feel them shifting
under the rug, like living things* —
to the years gather

in the darkening room.
Unchanging valley,
neighbourhoods of grass
but breath by breath
the bricks see out their owners,
there's nowhere
doesn't work its slow removal:
lean back

into yielding grass, the long
tree-lined avenues, take root
in the brick whisper, the flight
stored in the furniture,
the key as you turn it
slipping from hand to hand;
hesitate, linger, take what you can
from the opening door.

House for Sale

André Frénaud

So many have lived here, who loved
to love, to wake, dust, sweep the floor.
The moon's in the well and can't be seen.
The previous owners have disappeared
taking nothing with them.
The ivy swells in yesterday's sun.
The coffee stains and soot are staying put.
I fasten myself to mouldy dreams
and hug the grime of others' souls,
that mix of lace and plans gone wrong.
Concierge of failure, I'll buy the dump —
if it poisons me so be it, but never fear:
open the windows, put the sign on the lawn,
someone else will come in, sniff the air, begin again.

Whalefall

Every so often a windfall whale will blow through the depths
and where it lodges the pitchblack waters begin to stir,
specialists in their brilliant bodies to wake and move

towards their reward: a slow devouring, months of it,
the hagfish and rat-tails, crabs and sleeper sharks
picking the carcass clean until the bones collapse

but now the bone-world begins: *osedax*, the bone-eating worms
with their feathery plumes, blown like bubbles from the last
    whalefall
lock on and feed, generation after generation

until the place is empty again, a sulphide nothingness
the eggs have already fled, riding the currents for the fall
where it all goes on, the endlessly resisting life, the whale pulse.

Robert Graves House, Deià

That clarity,
how everything blazed
in the undaunted light
of itself.
A typewriter
nailed down
for all eternity,
drafts
a whisper from ink
flourishing their imperfections.
In the museum room
a looped film
of the artist shaving,
shelves of his books;
'I breed pedigree dogs
to feed my cats.'
The place held its breath.
In this readiness
what could resist?
Touch nothing but listen
for the lift-off, the print
of the house
on its own waiting,
the lucky lope
of the sleek black cat
through the ropes, and out.

Nando's Table

for Fernando Trilli

There was the turkey, *tacchino*, squabbling, impatient,
terrifying the hens and the gatecrashing pigeons

but that wasn't it.

There was the peacock, *pavone*, kingly
on the rooftop, in the branches, his tail dipped in grasses

but that wasn't it.

There was the family of goats, bearded, serious;
there was the cat in the piazza; there were chestnuts, fires

not those either, though nearly.

There was you in your sunglasses in the service station;
there was a necklace of beads; there were trees, avenues

and that was closer, but not exactly.

There was a long white road, almost, almost,
there was a table outside with wine and bread,

there was oil and cheese, a dish of lentils, as close
as you like now, the sun on the table, all of us eating,

all of us there as the lizards scuttled and the peacock
flew over and whatever we said has vanished

but the sun is somehow still on the table, the book
turned over, the oil softening the bread

and that must have been it, or something like it:

pane, olio, formaggio, sole

Nando's table washed with October,
all of us sitting there as if forever.

Cold

Maybe it's just
winter remembers winter
cold speaks to cold
but here it is again
in November
the ice-sharp town
the broken armies of trees
retreating along the canal
the nagging clarity

as if a journey had stalled
and must be found again
the paused place suddenly
resumed, revealing
bakery, corner, bridge
the further water
where a three-masted ship
permanently at anchor
noses the mist

and then it all opens out
on a square from Brueghel
the carts and lights
of a cold abundance
and my hands are running
the market-strewn
lit milk of your body
our breath turning to ice
to snag in the rigging

to hang in the trees
to lodge in every corner
of the prodigal town
cold speaking to cold
body to body so that

somehow the conversation
holds, the floorboards
come through again
the sharp edges of furniture,

you bend to light the stove
and I see how its flame is as wholly yours
as your bending to it
I see how things tend to you
winter luggage, a suitcase
in the hall, the guest in my voice
who never arrives
and maybe it's just
cold calls out to cold

that wrapped in winter I turn to you
your streets that have vanished
your house
that alone of its terrace survives
that on a breaking thread I pull
towards the brilliant centre
where the markets urge
and a cold festival
flares in our bones till we fall.

Delirium

Here drifts and falls, settles like snow
on the sill outside, and the floors of *now*
keep shifting from one absolute place
to another. It's as if

a hand has nudged her mind
from room to room through
cloudy neighbourhoods. Whose
furious life is this?

She knits
her bones of memory, turns
to her long dead husband
clear as day, and they argue the toss

unstoppably: everything here
is torrent and unending
till a forest grows round it
and the eyes are tangled and snared.

Now the room is full again, a thousand
ancient duties have returned,
a thousand fretting tasks
unticked and re-attached

as if all we thought we had survived
stays slotted in its air
to step towards us once more,
and who would have guessed

the terrible confidence of distress,
the persistence of rooms long left,
the clarity of so much held
raining around us like confetti . . .

Home

The room comes on
like another life, the alien

objects glitter, the fields outside
stretch into more than distance.

My own conversation
a thin hesitation you've long

decamped from. If I could believe
somewhere, unheard, unseen,

the unplayed music sounds,
the great distance loosens

and the undiluted life comes striding
giantly from the walls

but only silence comes
and frail music from the social room

only the objects sing
in their hard-tuned station

as you close your eyes
and melt back in.

'Death parks his car . . .'

Death parks his car and gathers his flowers and chocolates,
he writes his name in the visitors' book, drinks his tea and keeps
a full jug of squash in his room — permanent, unshiftable,
unmanna, unmiracle, the wine long spilled

on the road home from the feast. You feasted, or should have.
Now it's bingo, desultory conversation and a long look through
   the window;
now it's the architecture of containment
and the low skies of a midlands winter. No wonder

your hands tremble on the wheel as you leave the motorway
and take the slip road, the second exit on the roundabout,
the poorly signed country road. You park your car and gather
flowers, chocolates. The squash jug is full again. Sit back now

and dream of the coast, or not. Dream of your keys.

The Rooms

I CONTINUAL VISIT

Somehow a wilderness grows. The grasses
are full of small animals, the nights so absolute
you could haul yourself through blackness to the stars
and stream down like a stray god on the meadow.

The lake shifts and startles, a vixen cries from her lair.
The cottage veers and shakes and makes
like a mad thing for the trees. If there is a dog
he is barking now, shocked head pummelling air.

If there are foxes they are running, if the dead
have spilled from their fields they are here now
running headlong into the night. They are lost
and their gods with them, running down the narrow
lanes, leaping into hedgerows and ditches, mingling
with ash branches, rushes, the sleeping machines in their sheds.

To be loosed like that, streaming through the black countryside
or stopped somewhere, holed up in a ditch, stretched
on a bale under the whistling galvanize
as you forget the thin strands you died with

and darkness floats your whole life down, the whole span
settles on skin and hair, everything you were
like branches come together, a forest
of small touches. Here you are

yourself completely, so completely
your fingertips reach the lake,
your body drifts and falls like mist on the fields
and all your hours rain down . . .

There's not a blade of grass here that doesn't have your breath
    on it
before the sun burns you back to darkness again.

Who owns this land, these trees, these birds
pouring through the morning? I've come here
emptyhanded to harvest the wind on my face,
the secrecies of place. Star-gathering, lake-stalking

pilgrim head plugged in to draw the powers
out of what my leisure falls on

as tractors roar, lights come on in the yards
and machinery shreds the dark. Cattle
thunder past, a sheepdog barks
from the back of a jeep and a two-stroke engine
puts manners on the hedgerows. The whole
powered world is roaring its purpose

where silently I stand and focus my lens
on the bookish meadow with its subplot of swans.

The little jetty sinking in the rushes, hard to find.
Who has no house now will hang his hat
on the ramshackle, the provisional, a summer's

quick labour; will sit for hours inheriting a silence
stitched with warblers and lake tunes. Hermit
of the wetlands, sleep on reeds, sleep on water:

everything else can wait. The streets have flown,
the traffic vanished, and only the dark
comes on in the dark. Cock your ear and a tradition

opens: you can still get in, you can sing
until the edicts are unfrozen,
the palaces forgotten, until the dogs start barking

and the neighbour's Toyota comes creeping down the lane
to sniff you out and pin you down.

That it's all
exile and interlude, that the grass
escapes me, the implements hang heavy in my hands

that the roads are narrow but the wind is mine,
the wind and the rain and the big skies, the light
spilled and gathered, deck after deck of it

that all it amounts to is ash leaves, angles,
shapes and shifts, a forgetting
as the rain forgets itself and the lake repeats

the same first thought, that wherever we turn
is on its umpteenth rerun
that when it comes to earth or air or water

the miracle is the walking as if you'd never entered,
as if you'd never been there.

You could stand here passing things back and forth.
The rusted clasps snap open and from an old suitcase
years spill out. There's the tune
of a loose brass handle in a beloved door.
Through the window a cockcrow morning,
cold flags of a stone floor. The postman sits in the kitchen,
the train draws in to the summer station . . .

You could stand there, white-gloved and neutral
ensuring a constant flow. I'm sitting
in my grandfather's abandoned car
with my foot pressed down into the future.
I'm outside the door when the tyres crunch on the gravel,
shy hand raised like a gift or signal
searching for something to send back home.

I woke and thought
the place was a dream: house, lake, meadow
sharpening and shimmering like a doubtful gift
continually offered, continually withheld.
I could hardly walk to the end of the lane
without feeling my foolish life resist
the green song, the green light

as if every breath were not
a continual visit, every place the same gift;
as if the planet didn't sharpen and shimmer
and standing in the lane were not the offer
or as if whatever was resisted could be wrapped again
and like the missed song and the light forsworn
would endlessly return.

If we *could* go back and forth. If we could stand on the
    platform
with the summer ahead of us. If the small car
should renew itself and the road retrieve the journey,
the obedient trees retreat, reconfigure, sweep
down again to welcome us. The tin roof,
why not, falls back on the old shop,
a cold stream fills the bucket. It sways in the hand
spilling drops on the grass like a toll. Wherever
you look fills up and sways, the details
slip to their places. Everything is convinced. Inside
is the ache of furniture, the dreaming
bone-handled knives, blue willow dramas.
The meal is ready, the fêted guests tuck in. My hands
fly through the years, touching everything.

How lightly can you tread it, borrowed
earth, how long rest on reeds and water,
the birds and trees between their covers,
the firewood laboured, worked-up, the whole place
coming on as if concocted? Implements shine
like a consoling fiction; self-sufficiencies of rain,
of the light at the end of the lane,
drift through you, then fall to nothing.
All you can learn is to leave them alone.

All you can learn is to lean on the gable
and watch the lake call out to the sun.
All you can do
is stand back and listen to the darkness come.

So stand back. Listen. Let the darkness come.

Like something falling through you,
something happened on or woken with,
things begin to come. A summer suddenly
repeated and there you are, stretching to it.
Light falls from the side garden, the dogs
have all returned; the radio reaches back and pours
old shows into the kitchen and out
into the sunlit yard. Country music
haunts the rusted Escort, old news
persists; the skeins of gossip hold
and place after place comes on in my head: small
fierce broadcasts, the fields flourishing their one harvest,
a single ripple printing the lake, the voices
spilling into the sun as if the thing might stay on.

Where have we been? The window frames a possible garden
through which we seem to be walking. And even if
the place is empty, even if not a speck has travelled
there's no gainsaying the clarity of these trees, the tune
of the gravel and the hard grey sky of the gathering rain.
Something sends back print after print. The air
opens and there's a sudden reach from here to there,
the nape of your neck peals in the light.

The nape of your neck peals in the light
and I must be, must be gathered inside it
with some kind of tune. The words are sewn
into the stone wall; the shrubs, the slender gates
commemorate them, the sharpening air, our skin
like stone we carved ourselves on, and faded from.

2 HOUSED UNHOUSED

In the dream of perfect ownership
light drenches the wood, falling
through windows long looked through.
The wine and the oil sleep in the store
and small gods have come to rest
in hearth and threshold, tile and countertop,
in doors, in handles smooth from long use.
They inhabit radios, tumbling clothes,
the silence of the winter yard, and when we're here
they stream through us so every breath
is altar and core. Robed with home we go,
from room to room moving with grace,
lords of our little universe.

Who could forget the poet's house, the one he made
when he ran out of money and time
and what the world couldn't provide
he supplied himself, in verse after verse?
Remember the stonework, the avenues, the orchard?
Next came flowerbeds, the kitchen garden,
the wine cellar and the wood where every morning
he strolled for kindling. One river
led to another, a rusted gate grew meadows
where the autumn poured its aching light
and every evening he walked the boundaries
with calm affection, working the land
so hard in his mind when frost comes in April
we stumble from our beds, fearing for his vines.

This is the house that Jack lost, that packed up
and slid away, forgetting Jack and everyone else,
the faces, the photographs, breath on the mirrors,
prints on the bed, forgot hands, feet, fingertips
and so removed us that not a crack in the wall or a stain
in the floor remembered anything that came before.
Our uses passed, our noise fell back to whisper, rumour,
the age before silence gripped and held.
This is the absence the house proposes,
the emptiness we rush to fill when we enter,
eyes darting from corner to corner,
until we've hammered ourselves into it. This is the house
that Jack retrieved, hauling it back from ice-beds, oceans,
that he voiced, echoed, ghosted, that slips through his fingers
    still.

What do the places know? What do the rooms retain?
If there's a time when we might sink silently
into the hidden core, when the house
finally finds us out and comes to stay,
it must equally happen that unknown to us
the movers come and a slow
withdrawal enters the furniture, crawls
over the floors. We'll lean, unsteady,
against a countertop and see
that everything that matters has gone ahead
or stand helplessly, flailing at the tide,
as someone we love tries to put the key in the door
and tries again, and looks back, unhoused,
at the sudden strangeness of everything there.

Dream of me, the house inside the house, house
sneaking in to sleep under the skin, the stairs
under the stairs, the surface rising to the touch
from every surface; dream of the footscraper
outside the door, the march of a hundred shoes
shining with purpose, climbing through floors,
dream of the linen chest and the rims of glasses,
hands in the air, hands within hands, the memories
of bones, dream of the endless multiplication,
the children breaking out from us to play their games
and rain their voices down. Their faces are assembled
in the frames again, their unvanished smiles look out
at the filling space, in the dream where past after past
has come to roost, and everything has returned.

There is never one place to go to or come back from.
We might stay forever in a shifting room,
as if we crossed a river on driftwood —
someone throw us a line from the secure bank,
someone guide our steps across the lumber —
or fall from room to room in a broken house
where days drift into each other with small separation.
Lapped at, lifted, the floors move. Is this us
standing in the hall, watching everything familiar
peel, unstick? The walls stretch and thin, we're blown
from house to house down tunnels of silk. Every
life reaches in, every garden remembers our touch,
every photograph lifts from its frame
and comes running toward our open arms.

Pack the walls away, let this be the room
from rock chair to rock pool from breaking surf
to quicksilver shallows
from the boat-shaped house yearning on the headland
to the graveyard island hard and clear
as if you might measure a distance
from falling stones to spreading dunes and across the grass
to the wooden gate where the whole summer

has come to rest
                            all childhood gathers on the bars
swings inward to whatever's wished for
as now with every step a lightening and at the end

the delicate unlikely gardens we linger in
a hand here an eye there drawing it together —
let this for once hold and compose us.

The house washed out of you like a tide.
As you sat in your chair the wood
released your grip, the keys melted away.
Light poured through the window
and heat from the radiator filled the room
but the cold gathered, the doors
forgot your touch. A hand moves
to sign a contract, the language
returns to its vault and the bench
rots quietly in the garden or is sanded,
varnished, weather-proofed to take
the no less reliable sun, the no less
indifferent rain. What must be here,
what could any of us have taken
that wouldn't slip through the fingers,
what could we have left behind that if
out of the blue we came back, gusting
through the open doors, might still
move towards us, remembering?

The map dissolves, the house falls down.
Who, ever, is really at home? Live
in the cracks, in the creak of salvage;
where the ship lies snagged on the broken roof
and the years lie ripped in the fields.
Live in the tune in the car-radio afternoon,
give it its shrine, with the hand taken, the satchel
safely brought home and the homework done.

Wrap nothing round you but what you'll never own;
the winds are ready, the waves honed,
the secret in the body about to be disclosed.
Live where you can, in the clear-strained wine,
the harvest of a single breath
streaming bubbles in the yard . . .

3 DRIFT

I woke on the avenue and made my way
till the lime trees yielded to the solid brick
and I found the old imposing door
then waited for the ancient servant the scene
demanded, sallow and hoary handed,
longhaired and stooped, cranky
and put upon but no one came,
the door when it opened opened itself,
no creaking or fuss, a mild inward sigh.
This is the house your life has built,
open your eyes and enter it and I did
and it closed again and it came to me
I was stuck here now unscripted and afraid.

I opened my eyes and turned
into silence, sunlight, objects crowded, sharp, the sharpness
things pull on when we take them in. Out
of the rocking horse a spill of straw, out of the clock
the remembered tune, props of a lifetime
polished and shown. A flight of albums
raced through the years. I pushed them aside
and lurched through the clutter, knocking
cupboards, TV sets, insistent toys, infinite
gothics of memory like a hand closed over a candle
snuffing out the flame. I closed my eyes
and refused to move, as if that stillness were the exit
from the prison of stuff and the hands that hold it.

I woke in darkness, someone else's,
someone's night into which I'd slipped like a draught
and lay like nothing, unbodied, unselfed, an interval
the quiet collected in, a ditch
scooped from time or a chamber
under the skin of the earth where I sewed
my breath to the mouths of the dead,
where the pulse of what I'd left
echoed faintly from deep below, then
grew stronger until whatever place it was
was filled with it and I knew
everything that had ever lived was beating there
and I'd sleep forever in the din.

Unloosed now, adrift, I woke
in my mother's arms, in her angry eyes
as she stared at the wall, stared at me
and turned back in, and I crept and crawled
in the broken room of her mind.
Everything leeched from the day, the world
was this room lit by a current of panic.
The pathways close down, the signs fall and don't
come up again, there's somewhere I wanted
to go but the map of my life is cinders.
Sit with me in the uncharted room, whoever
you are, or take to the hills with your bags
and keys, no photographs, no light begging from the field
or words from strangers crying to be held.

The door opened and more doors behind and more
behind those and in each room a table
with a meal in progress: I could smell lamb, chicken,
fish, an assault of soups and the fumes
of half a vineyard and from each table
someone turned to look, raising a glass
and beckoning, pointing to the empty place.
When the doors closed what I couldn't forget
was how there'd been such ease in it,
such a relieving lightness in the dissolving,
the self dividing, how we'd flocked
to the calling tables, and sat and ate and talked
to the living and the dead and looked across
at ourselves looking back, smiling, raising a glass.

That was one room, this is another
where no one ever stands still, station concourse
or airport terminal, where all the different
wanderers go their wholly separate ways
and would sooner raise a fist than a glass
if they happen on each other, so fixed,
so locked in the inviolable journey.
Whichever one I am, the watcher,
the self between assignments checking his ticket
in the interstitial zone, finds a bench
and sits still before the tannoy crackles out
a name, a place, and I take my seat
in the carriage, not speaking, not wanting
to meet the eyes of the strangers there.

Think of all the places you've lived in
and as they converse and build their house
think too of all the places you've never been,
the great assemblies where you haven't stood,
the billion roll calls your name is absent from.
Creep up the drainpipe of the house set
in too many flats, try the couch, the hot plate,
look for your letters on the floor. This
room collects them all, disposes
its inventory of the unexplored.
Crawl into your neighbour's bed, it's here
with the scattered fences of the district,
the torn maps of the world, the held
breath of what was possible once.

Something's cooking here: chicken curry, late July
I saw
piled up shoes, forgotten carpets,
the ants of Tritonville Avenue still organized, triumphant.
Here we lay . . . my elbow breaks a glass
I come on now, still deliciously shattering.
In my arms a heartbreak of laundry . . .
Wrested
from the four corners of the room
table legs and old beds
and here you come with the steaming bowl,
the strap climbing back onto your shoulder,
your mouth opening to say, all
this ancient pleasure, what exactly do you want it for?

In the room too late arrived at my dead father waits.
I shut the door behind me, open his eyes
and step by step I take him back. It's not too late
or if it is I've spun the arguments, swept the boards
with lyre and longing and now trawl home
to the living room with the hospital bed, then that
goes and the wheelchair melts and the stick flies off
and sea and sand come pouring in, we slouch
against the prom wall and suck our cones, then
shift again where haycocks stand in June sun,
the hay pricking the small of our backs
when we sit to rest and drink our milk
and I've looked too hard or the angle's wrong
or I can't find the instructions and when I do he's gone.

Lay your nose against the earth
and sniff the dead back up, their
loose limbs and bubbly talk.
The deeper you go the better the tunes,
this room the darkest, deepest, farthest from air
exploding with song, but there's only one layer
no further border
                    I keep remembering
beside the coffin his favourite paper, a bottle of beer.
Reachable world!
                    Death is always yesterday
its cities built of paper a single spark from fire.
If we came back we'd come crushing through the earth
as through the lightest, thinnest door . . .

Everything in this room is exactly as you left it,
the self-assembly furniture disassembled, the pictures
piled on the floor. The light pours in
as if it too might be taken down, broken up
and packed away. Open it up,
take it out again, with everything we did,
the whole lost city of our love. Nothing
quite goes away, nothing's ever really undone,
you haven't just walked into this room,
what happened is
you never found your way out, and the city
you thought you'd never see again
keeps leaking in. Outside, always, the doubling street,
the secret square inside the square.

The roar of the sea below the grassy hill.
The lute pouring through the open door.
No one has heard them, no one is there.
The ash trees hugging the backlit river.
The nothing river, the unseen trees.
The bicycle by the cabin door.
The dog curled up on the balcony steps.
The music left out in the rain.
Somewhere in the woods a leaf, a cry.
The shale loose on the mountain top.
The brickwork of the chimney breast.
The pause in the radio as it collects itself.
The untrawled depths, the farthest star.
Anything. Anywhere. Anyone. Not you.

I went in, sat down, saw the place
had already been taken possession of,
the perfected other, elbow on the mantelpiece,
standing in front of a blazing life.
He didn't sing, but I knew if he did
the walls would melt, the furniture sigh.
Or speak, but pleasure streamed from his face
and love came pulsing through the air.
I knew if I stayed I could reach for it,
everything gnarled and angered would fall away.
I could feel whatever I was drifting out
and didn't stir to call it back, not wanting
to flounder continually in the same current, or settle
for the wave when the ocean crooked its thumb.

for Dennis O'Driscoll

A room for you where poetry comes
Holub Miłosz Hölderlin Brecht

the door wide open for miraculous draughts
the rivers washing through us to where they began

the glacier roar of the white Himalayas
amusing themselves in their icy solitude

and the misery of lost poets parading
in darkness looking for the arms of the gods.

The slow spin of the reel to reel
catches the gravelly voice, the reedy voice, the thunder

down the mountain voice and all the questions after
but uncatchable now your own: the mike brings

not you but the poems shaking themselves loose
drifting up the stairs and in till the room is filled with them.

Lines from a Victorian Photographer

Paul Martin, Yarmouth, 1892

She lies in the sand as if she'd risen from it,
as if the sand had dreamed her dress
and elaborated
her pinned up hair, her sculpted hat.

He leans over her
dark-suited, composed
having stepped outside his century
as if for a moment and travelled down

still bowler-hatted and immaculately shod,
his umbrella still perfectly rolled
and lying now beside her
to await the outcome.

*

He has conjured her maybe
though not so much as she has taken him.
The sand is in every fold of her dress,
she lies in the sand, the sand lies in her

and she is smiling: there is nothing of him
she doesn't comprehend, the brim of his hat
knows more than he does
and travels farther.

*

Around them a world moves,
someone else's,
a procession of dark dresses escorting children,
boats conquering the foreshore,

a solitary chair
that has somehow wandered out
to take the air and suitably refreshed will return
to its great affairs.

*

Now they have fallen deeper,
they have disappeared into the mantelpieces
nightstands and abandoned chests, they are gazing out
like cathedrals of themselves

where the light took hold of them,
raised them up, wiped them down
and disposed them for the future
but missed

their true flourishing
where disbelieving the arrangement they tumbled
out of the frame to attempt
instead a fallen kiss, a dishevelment.

Hardware Store

Jean Follain

In a country hardware store
men come to buy
screwdrivers and wrenches
their hair is grey their hair is red
neatly flattened or flying wild.
A bluish air fills the serious spaces,
into its iron tang women set loose
the scent
of themselves.
Just to touch the spotless bolts and drills
is to feel the irresistible
weight of the world.

The hardware store floats towards the stars
selling, until no one wants for them,
nail after dazzling nail.

Lines for Borges

Eternity settles in your bones, blows you
from one dark corner to another. No surprise
that night after night you come to rest
in a suburb on the outskirts you hardly recognize,

the needle tilting to walls washed blue,
a shady fig tree, a crumbling path. History
trumpets from the statuary,
the streets shuffle their names like cards

and the phone rings out in Government Buildings.
It might be the afterlife, its empty squares
and unanswering lights, its smell of Buenos Aires,
Alexandria, Dublin, all labyrinths and mirrors

in which the world grows old, then suddenly young,
every moment no sooner fled than aching to begin.
Or you've somehow pushed through the sky
to look back at the repeating fathers

walking from the graveyard
with their fathers on their arms, childhood
climbing through the eucalyptus air,
the constant river waiting for your step.

Whoever crosses it is not you,
yet here you are, washed out
to a starry estuary, and here's the source
that spills you back to earth to build

your time-denying dam again. *And yet, and yet*
time is what we're made of,
we toss in its chains and sing
what leaves us behind. Walls washed blue,

the shape of a coastline, the iron
rush of love and the body falling
unconsoled to where the bones spill
in the hourglass whispering

The world, unfortunately, is real . . .

The Capsule

When it came to it, nothing we wanted would fit.
We stood on the road and packed what we could,

the tickets and music and sealable wit,
whatever we had, whatever thought good.

What we should have offered we couldn't transmit:
the flare of a season, the sunlit wood.

We sent you the tomb, but the body had fled,
we stood by the window and watched the light flit,

we reached out to take it but wrapped up instead
the pages and proofs, the buckle and kit.

When you open the capsule and examine what's in it
consider what isn't; for all that we had,

as we fiddled with clasps, as we stood on the road,
when it came to it, nothing we wanted would fit.

The Table

As if everything has been tending
towards this
completeness: the bread rolls, the pitcher of wine,
the shared meat and the conversation
indivisible, where outside

is a distant planet, the border beyond the table
barely imaginable, and there's no
intenser city than now,
our delicate companionship come to rest
on a last toast, a coffee

before the world swarms in
and bears us off;
as if it's all
in the dispersal,
not in what comes together

but what bubbles and evaporates
and we're so much here
because what the waiters bear
along with the laughter and the perfect agreement
is our absence,

the table cleared and wiped down,
the fresh glasses and cutlery
untouched by us,
the long streets and the journeys home,
the silence of our never finding this place again

and a last drink with which to toast the table, the dispersal.

Elbow Room

for Joe Connolly

A letter brings me to my teenage father,
unpicks his bones and calls him back
from his week of boarder's rations, his years
of darkness and silence, to where he sits
in the depths of winter in his cousins' kitchen
and wolfs his Sunday lunch.

What does he say? He lifts a fork and vanishes
until now, how many winters
later, and his father, too, lifted and returned
to drive his hackney down the narrow roads
flat capped and with his elbow out the window
so close I can reach my hand across —

as if that casual elbow opened a portal,
poked through time to graze the city air
or as if I might somehow reach in to raise
these always resisting bones, always
unfinishable journeys. How much can you stretch
from lunch to dinner, from headstone to hearth

and back again? But the engine is running
in the unkillable car, my grandfather changes up
as he leaves the bend
and accelerates from the letter.
Around the corner, my father drains his cup,
pushes back his chair. After lunch

comes nothing, unmemory, unwritten.
I can follow them to nowhere, to where
the engine rusts and the broken years
lie in fields, and when the traffic stalls

I can open the window
and rest my arm on the door, let my elbow

graze the zone, let the altered day come in.

The Night House

The windows are nothing, the doors are blank, the sun is
    washed from the brick
but at night the routes return, the games pull back, the streets

stretch and open. A confusion of trucks and competing
    furniture,
the strained backs of the movers, but by nightfall the dust
    has settled,

the castors have dented the floor: everything has always
    been here.
The mouse inherits his flesh, the cheese turns fresh, a hand

has pulled the signals from the sky. All day the unstoppable
    networks
but at night you turn the knob and wait in the silence for
    the snow to clear.

All day the contract waiting, the deeds in their box, the
    compliant maps
but at night the carpets laid, the wallpaper rolled and the
    milkfloats loaded.

At night the coalmen sit with their sacks in the hall, the
    postman juggles his years,
and the feet released from darkness fleshed, shod, listen,
    coming up the stairs again.

Listener

A gust of grief
as I lock my bike to its metal hoop
and stand on the pavement
solid as a tree

listening to news of the future
from a shop radio
pierced by infrastructure
the great projects

coiling under the streets and running
past the backs of houses not yet built
the rumble in this day's core
of all the machinery

that won't sustain me
and that I seem
suddenly avid for
claw, hammer, the gaping

tunnels, thunderous
tracks, all the frequencies
the secret listener, flown from me,
long ago tuned to.

Habitable Zone

for the planet Kepler 22b

So much to infer
from the flicker, the measurable dip
in the shine of a star.
Something's there,
climbing the bulletins:
oceans and valleys, bronzed mountains,
the kind of absence into which
the guessed at
are about to come
flitting from the shadows
or carrying the fiery tablets down.

So far to reach
we plunge right in
like divers down to kingdoms
unimagined,
we hold it to our ears like a conch
for gods to whisper in or the songs
a sun might sing. Wanting
anything but ourselves
who laid cold hands on all we knew
and spun our gift
like a gambler's coin.

A pale blue planet turns in the mind
climbing out of darkness to lie
its quiet body close.
We feel its breath
on our necks, fall asleep
to the swish of water
and when we wake
we climb out from our shelters
and stretch our faces to the rising star . . .

Poem Beginning with Two Lines by André Breton

The wardrobe is filled with linen,
there are even moonbeams I can unfold.
The roof has slipped back on the gables,
old trees march in from the cold.

The wardrobe is filled with linen,
the beds are slept in again.
Out of the air spill table and chairs,
the wine has crept back to the rim.

The wardrobe is filled with linen,
the drawers are packed with days.
The cabinet lies unsmashed in its corner,
there's a harvest of sun on the floor.

The wardrobe is filled with linen,
the shadows come back to the wall.
They've gone to collect the children
from the strangers who stand in the hall.

The rooms are empty and cold,
the drawers are littered with bones.
The wardrobe is filled with linen
no one can touch or unfold.

Dress

How hard it would be
just to let things go on: the unwatched sun,
the unfussed rain, the outgrown dresses
an unregarded chain link by link
settling on the floor . . .
Today I reached for the camera
to get you pirouetting in the new one,
a minute of pure joy I was terrified to miss.
Oh, I know. But you close your eyes
and a thousand sleeps go by,
you come down the stairs
from your powerful kingdom,
speaking the language, occupying the space,
wrapping the house around you
and all I want is to find the word
that turns the body down, slows the bones,
and breaks the link in all the chains, the one
that keeps you twirling and singing
in a lens of delight. Of course, of course
forget all this, I'd want nothing less.
Jump into your skin, into dress after dress,
put the language on, the music,
stretch into every one of your days,
I'll try not to notice, or learn
to turn my blindness into praise.

Harm

Houla, Syria, 2012

Whoever enters kneels to wash
blood from hair and faces, untangle limbs,
then staying in the wreckage, lodged
like a guardian there, lifts the bodies up,
carries them back to the miracle desks
and watches as the eyes forget their shock
and the songs find their way back

but then, because the deaths are endless,
must see it happen over and over
the place rent with cries, the faces
twisted, the disbelieving eyes; must watch
the blood return, small things find their harm again,
a yellow jumper, yellow scarf, a pink
diamanté belt, and reach and reach for the useless cloths.

Quiet

A legion of dogs has passed the window
unregarded, unhowled at
and cats come swaggering
into the noiseless garden.
Is there no watchfulness left
in the ruined couch, the stained glass?
And where did all this quiet come from?
Secretly the house collected it
and releases it now like a slap.
I bite on an apple and nothing happens.
Silence bounds into the kitchen
and lifts its black eyes.
How is it possible
the popped-up toast can sit in the toaster
and not rouse you, the stairs
not explode at the scrape of butter?
Undisputed, unaccompanied
the slices wait.
Where are your ten imploring years?
From foot to foot I shift
while south of here
in unfamiliar territory
your curious hungry ashes scatter,
scour the woodland and the wind
and snatch this quiet from my hands.

Lifeguard

I only just resist
calling you back from where you're dancing
on the farthest, edgiest rock

as when you swim beside me
out of your depth, fearless,
I want to pull you in

and you laugh, pointing to the island,
a moored boat bobbing, anything
miles out and inviting.

Or I'm standing on the beach, watching you
race in and plunge,
throwing you line after invisible line

as if this were my calling, to patrol nervously,
to stand on a shore
and feel my body wheel to wherever you are

to pluck caution from the wind
and offer it to you like a gift
and hear your laughter hurl it back.

You swim farther out, my lines are tangled,
my whole body's a flailing net.
Yet all this

fearful churning, I also want to say
what a useless gift it is
when what you need is my unseeing eye

when what we're here to reach for
is always where the islands are
always the unguarded shore.

Elegy

For Frantz the craftsman whose craft
was the breaking of bones
who lifted the heavy cartwheel
and brought it down on the outstretched limbs
thirty seven blows to kill a man
and wrote everything down
because that too was order and care
in a single decade
two hundred and twenty eight despatched
one hundred and ninety one flogged
five finger choppings three ear clippings
one tongue snipping
prostitutes, procuresses
poachers, perjurers
once, his own brother-in-law
and the responsibility vested in him
for all preliminary torture
an honest man
upright, brave, pious
the cleanser
of Nuremberg making his way
in a difficult world
retiring finally
after a botched burning
who loved to heal
fifteen thousand patients
he said three imperial emissaries
one Teutonic knight, Bamberg's
cathedral provost
all manner of injuries
efficiently cured
here lies
in honourable quiet
Frantz Schmidt, physician.

Audience with BB

Lie down, now, wait
for summer: the rum's
bought, the guitar re-strung
let white shirts
flutter in sun . . .

* * *

Remember this?
Pull the chairs round again,
fill the glasses:

* * *

WHEN THE BLUE WIND OF EVENING WAKES GOD THE FATHER
he sees the sky above him whiten, and likes it.
Then the great cosmic chorus delights his ears:

the cry of flooded forests about to drown,
the frail wooden houses groaning under the weight
of too much furniture and too many people . . .

* * *

And the misery of Bert Brecht, who isn't too well . . .

* * *

Well, I wasn't.

* * *

Still, though, the crazy *Lieder*

of the waters rising in the forests,
the soft breath of the sleeping
snug in their old deal beds,

the ecstatic babble of the cornfields
pouring out their hearts in prayer,
the great words of great men . . .

*

And the brilliant songs of Bert Brecht, who isn't too well.

*

And I'm not, but thank you.

*

Coming out of the darkness with chairs
and questioning faces, quietly
they assemble on the riverbank.
The evening
alive with expectation.
Cigarettes like fireflies, the clink
of miraculous glasses.

*

I want a poem
like a shoe —
Empedocles' shoe,
have you seen it?
The shabby, palpable
earthly shoe
he aimed at the undergrowth

as he stood
on the edge of the crater
before he plunged
into legend, rumour.
The only thing left,
the relic undoing the miracle,
the clue
to an unasked question
insisting only on itself
the shabby, palpable
earthly shoe . . .

*

Things come back
sometimes mysteriously,
the biting blade of memory
troubling the skin of the desired
or invented. These borders
are poorly patrolled . . .

*

THE MORNING'S SOBER PARTING: COOL
on the threshold she stood, coolly looked at.
Then I saw a single strand in her hair was grey
and stopped short, suddenly unable to go.

Unspeaking I held her, and when she asked
why the guest wouldn't leave
now his night was over, as we had agreed,
I looked at her candidly and answered:

one more night, one more night I'll stay,
make the most of the time. The truth is your standing
there on the threshold has stirred me.

But whatever we say let our talk be quick
for we both forgot that you are dying.
Then desire overwhelmed me and I couldn't speak.

*

A stir in the audience
Yes, I'm here, returning your stare
threshold to threshold. What
stirs now? Candidly
I take you in, candidly
open the door, my snow-white bones and ashen hair.

*

What
do you want from me?
Have you brought me here
to see how the world has changed?
You wrote for us, posterity says,
why should you complain if we write to you?

*

I move, I sit, I sleep.
I put my coat on and take it off again.
I contradict myself. I write the gospels
of rivers and trees . . .

*

IN PALE SUMMER WHEN THE GENTLEST WIND
stirs in the trees there's nothing to do
but stretch out in rivers or pools
like plants or waterweed where pike lurk.
Our weightless bodies fall from us
and if an arm should break the water,
straying into the light above, the wind
will take it for a branch and rock it.

The noon sky is hugely still.
You close your eyes as swallows pass.
The mud is warm: when the water bubbles
we know a fish has just swum through us.
My body, my thighs, my resting arm
still in the still river, come together
when the cool fish swim through us,
the sun gleaming over the water . . .

When evening comes and the lazy
body stirs and your limbs begin to ache
forget it, don't even look back, throw
all that into the blue waters streaming fast.
It's best to hang on until evening
for it's then the sharkpale sky comes
ravening above rivers and riverbanks
and everything shines sharp in its light.

Time then to lie on your back
in the usual way, time to float
but not to swim, just to lie flat
on grit and gravel, as if you belonged to them,
time to examine the sky and sink down
as if into a woman's arms, without
effort, as God himself does
when he swims in his rivers at nightfall.

*

and

*

WHEN YOU CLIMB UP FROM YOUR EVENING BATHING
naked and with your skin tingling
find the highest trees and climb them
in the light wind when the sky is pale.
Look for the great trees that in the evening
gravely rock their highest branches
and wait in the leaves until darkness falls,
bats and nightmares pressed to your brow.

Your back will sting
as you squeeze between the branches.
Painfully you'll continue, climbing
higher into the tree. If you like
you can rock yourself on it
but do it delicately: be to the tree
as its own treetop,
a hundred years of evenings . . .

*

That was the gospel of rivers and trees.

*

We live in our moment
shuffling through the ruins

from ruined city to ruined city
carrying unreliable news

dust reporting dust
ashes surveying ashes

hungry bones come up
to see what remains

                    *

If only history could follow us here:
the black, obliterating night,
the all-consuming, all-concealing wood.
Here the tanks collapse, the drones forget,
the rockets and the rifles quietly rust.
Having gorged on meat and brandy
Cortés and his men lie where they fell.
When they wake at noon
the forest will have grown through them,
they'll hear the faint bellowing of the oxen
like a tide going out forever.
Lost to each other, they'll flounder.
The forest drops its veils. History
will be the last breath
of the conquistador and his crew,
the sky and the sun,
the blood-spread centuries
removing themselves from view.

                    *

There are things I need to recover.
There are times I need to pull over
on the hard shoulder of desire.

                    *

What was her name?

*

ON A DAY IN BLUE SEPETEMBER
under a plum tree I held her
silently in my arms, my pale
still love like a sweet dream.
Above us the summer sky
drifting a vast white cloud
I stared at long, but when
I turned to look again had gone.

Since then how many Septembers
have drifted by, the plum trees
long cut down, and you ask me
what became of that love?
I honestly can't remember.
I understand the question but
of her face remember nothing.
I only know I kissed it once

and would have forgotten that
if it weren't for the cloud, so white
and immense above us, so perfectly
clear before me still. The plum trees
for all I know are blooming now
and she has borne her seventh son.
Yet the cloud for only minutes bloomed
and when I looked again was gone.

*

*The cloud has come back, it is here now
and willing to speak. Well, cloud,*

raise a woolly hand and swear.
The cloud speaks: this is the man,
this the girl, these are the photographs.
As you see, no plum trees. Her
fine features, her name
pouring through the hedgerows.
Here nothing is forgotten, your arms
cradle her stone limbs. Everything
that is solid, immovable, permanent
has come to rest here. White
and immense you float
above yourself, forever looking down.

*

The drowned Ophelias come,
climbing up the banks
and crossing the miles of fields
to take their places:

*

WHEN THE DROWNED GIRL DESCENDED
from the streams to the widening rivers
the opal sky shone brilliantly
as if to appease her floating body.

River weeds and algae clung to her
and slowly pressed her down, cold
fish touched her limbs, reeds
and animals weighed down her last journey.

The evening sky was black as smoke
but it held its stars like torches above her

and the dawn was clear, that she might have
the span of one more day from light to dark.

When her pale body rotted in the water
it seemed that little by little God forgot her:
first her face, then her hands and at last her hair
till she was one more corpse in the corpse-filled river.

*

Metropolis! Metropolis!
Come all you
culchies, bogmen, townies
and listen to my advice
what your mother told you
is strictly for the birds
leave your contract in your pocket
it won't be honoured here
go and learn your ABC
the ABC is no one
gives a shit about you here
but don't be discouraged.

*

If ever you meet your parents
as you stroll around the town
remember this
say nothing to them, turn the corner
pull the hat they gave you
right over your face
always cover your tracks

remember: say what you like
but don't say it twice

and if someone else
mouths your thoughts, be sure
to deny them, remember this
no one can touch
the man who signed nothing
left no photo
never logged on
ignored the petition
who wasn't there
who never said a word
but covered his tracks

and make sure when you die
no tombstone betrays
the place where you lie
remember this: let no
chiselled script shout out
time and date and place
for one last time
cover your tracks

*

Sock it to us!
We want the dark forests, the asphalt streets!
Mahagonny! Chicago! Berlin!

*

I, BERTOLT BRECHT, COME FROM THE DARK FORESTS

*

Yes, that's the one! Give that to us!

I can't, I'm sorry.

Yes, you can. Go on!

*

I . . .

*

I, BERTOLT BRECHT

*

That's it!

*

I, BERTOLT BRECHT, COME FROM THE DARK FORESTS

*

Ah!

*

My mother brought me to the cities
as I lay inside her, and as long as I live
the chill of the forests will live in me.

*

We knew you had it in you!

*

And so forth. You know how it was.
I had everything. I smiled at everyone.
I was, I am unreliable. The pine trees pissed,
the foul birds kept up their racket . . .

＊

What will remain of these cities
is what went through them: the wind.

In the convulsions to come I can only hope
bitterness won't let my cigar go out,
I, Bertolt Brecht, carried in the womb to the asphalt cities
out of the dark forests long ago.

＊

We like our poetry
big and swaggery.
The dark theatre of the poem!
The proud flourish of the name!
The pissing trees, the avian racket . . .
Let's sit him on our knees and chat,
let's try and keep his cigar alight.

＊

TWO HARD THINGS
teaching without students
reading without applause.

＊

I have not been sleeping.

*

THE OLD DREAM AGAIN: THE MARKET'S COLLAPSED
I can't shift a thing, the wolf
is lunging through the door.
Outside the fishmonger is speaking in tongues

and my friends and relations look through me
as if they'd never seen me before.
The woman I slept with for seven years
nods politely on the landing, and passes me by.

I know all the rooms are empty, I know
the furniture has vanished, the mattress is slashed
and the curtains have been ripped from the windows.
No effort has been spared: I walk into the yard and see

my washing fluttering on the line
though as I look closer I can see
a new patch here, an extra button there — it seems
I've moved. Someone else is living here now,

buttoning my shirt in the gloom, reaching
for my shoes . . .

*

SEPTEMBER AGAIN, THE WOMEN QUEUING
for schoolbooks and copies.
Despairingly they fish the last pennies
from battered purses, outraged

at the price of knowledge. If they only knew
how unreliable it was, all this learning

wrapped tenderly on a kitchen table
and handed to their children.

*

How well do you know yourselves?
Do you have any idea
what knowledge floods in
when things get difficult?
We did see that man
and he did flag us down
as we drove in the rain
in our comfortable saloon.
He begged us to take him.
We could have done it,
there was room enough
but yes, it was my voice
objecting. *We can't take anyone.*
Later, in the mirror, in
the safe house, the new
knowledge, the newly
configured room stared back.

*

WIRKLICH ICH LEBE IN FINSTEREN ZEITEN!

*

They won't say
When the cherry trees blossomed in Rathgar
but *When the bondholders crushed the workers*
They won't say

When the boy spent all day skimming stones
but *When they were fine-tuning the drones*
They won't say
When she glided into the room
but *When the great powers twiddled their thumbs*
And they won't say
The times were dark
but *Where was the poets' tune?*

                *

The poets in the audience shift uneasily.
Art resist, put out your brightly coloured stall.
The hunter drones take off, that only kill
'in single digits' only those
likely to be reasonable targets. Obviously
the technology is improvable.
The poets calibrate the reach of elegy.
Obviously it is
a flawed technology. Art receive
our attentive outrage, robotics of grief.

                *

From exile we come
and to exile return.
What else is this place?

                *

Svendborg: the years of exile.
Svendborg: the poet snug beneath his thatch
listening to the news, despatching his own
blood-haunted bulletins:

WHEN THE POLITICIANS TALK OF PEACE

the dogs in the street know
war is on the way

when the politicians condemn war
the order to mobilize has already been given.

*

CHALKED ON A WALL
They want war.
Whoever wrote it
is silent now.

*

I wasn't alone. In dark times
no poet is at home. Besides,
where did Homer live, or Dante?
Not to mention Li Po and Tu Fu
shuffling through the war zones
where millions died.

Euripides, too, packed his bags
and even the dying Shakespeare
they tried to gag.
Nor was it just the muses
chased François Villon.

He may have been beloved
but still Lucretius fled
as Heine did, and look

I dangle my cigar from exiled lips
and hang my hat
on a Danish hook.

*

Emigrants, you call us,
as if we had a choice
but we didn't wander out
to hang our hats on foreign hooks.
We fled. We are
the displaced and proscribed
and the land that took us in
is exile, not home.
One day when things are better
we'll return. We've forgotten
nothing, we've forgiven
nothing. We know what they do.
Even here the cries reach us.
We slouch down the corridors
like rumours of crime,
our breath is evidence, our
broken shoes. This is not
the last word. One day
we will return . . .

*

HOW ARROGANT IT SEEMS
to be making poems now.
I look with delight
at apple blossoms
and the tyrant's ravings
fill my mind.

Only then
do I march to my desk.

*

IT'S NIGHT
the couples
are asleep. The women
will give birth to orphans.

*

*It's spring in the world, things
are looking up. The snows release
their grip, the heart . . .*

*

FOG DESCENDS ON
the road
the poplars
the farmsteads
and
the artillery

*

MY YOUNG SON ASKS ME:
should I study maths?
What for, I want to say.
That two hunks of bread
are more than one
you'll find out soon enough.
My young son asks me:
should I study French?

What for, I want to say.
That empire's done for. Run
your hand across
your stomach and groan,
no one will mistake you.
My young son asks me:
should I learn history?
What for, I want to say.
Learn how to stick
your head in the sand,
then you might survive.

Yes, I tell him, learn maths,
learn French, learn history!

*

The ruined cities come together,
debris and limbs, blood haunted
brightly patterned clothes, the same
unrelenting figures scouring the rubble
the same bricks, the same stones

the same knowledge used again
once washed, twice washed, so scrubbed
and scraped, so rinsed and cleansed
the stink and rot are almost gone
brick by brick, bone by bone

the ruined cities rise
the schoolroom songs ring out
the old books are taken down
and quietly across the pristine rags
the old stains spread again.

*

No writer is an island,
least of all me.
I open my mouth
and dozens fall out.

*

Help me, flag me down
stop the car and take me out
take my place, let me wander

through the forest
towards some bright city
history has forgotten, or having woken
rubbing harmless sleep from its eyes
is just about to enter.

*

I SIT AT THE SIDE OF THE ROAD
as the driver changes the wheel.
I don't much like where I've come from,
I don't much like where I'm going.
Why, then, am I watching so eagerly
as he changes the wheel?

*

AND I ALWAYS THOUGHT: SIMPLIFY
or lose it. When I tell the truth
things should smash, the planet falter,
the heart be torn to shreds.
Don't you know

if you don't resist you're done for?

*

THE PLAY'S OVER, THE ACTORS SPENT. SLOWLY
like a sagging gut the theatre empties.
In the dressing room
the stink of mimicry and stale rhetoric
is washed off with the make up and sweat.
At last the lights go down, leaving
in darkness the bungled mess, the lovely
nothing of the tormented stage.
In the empty stalls, in the audience-whiff,

the insatiable playwright sits
remembering everything . . .

*

You liked it here, didn't you? he said, and I nodded,
watching the cloud shadow darken the mountain
although what did it solve, who did it save?
The sea shrank the beach to a finger
and still the waves came in, nearer and nearer.
He flicked his ash on the sand, shaded his eyes.
Summer's here, you think I don't remember?
And still the sun pours down on chaos, terror.
Choose between the gunfire and the weather
or get them both: fly to the cursor, curl up in paper,
wear out the desk with risk after risk.

Epilogue: Words for BB

As always
it's a bad time for poetry.
The stars don't listen, the bored

dust swirls, the tin-eared dead
have turned away. What
can you do?

Burned by a committee of suns
or drenched by endless rains
you pull your hat down and trudge

from the traumas of the mountains
to the troubles of the plains . . .
Or you have settled despite yourself

for a windswept exile, sailboats
in a sound and the muffled thunder
of empires on manoeuvres.

It's spring again, or it's always spring:
the tree you planted
and half-heartedly watered

now rakes the sky and darkens
a continent. Everything monstrous
has somehow survived:

tyrants enough to keep you awake
and chain you to your desk,
eternal gunfire ripping the dark.

Worse still, though, to persuade you back,
pull the darkness open and sail you
somehow gently down: *What*

did I tell you? Everything
alters but nothing changes:
with your dying breath you can

begin again, but the world you leave
is the one you made, the blood
you spilled is a hardened stain.

From the dark forest
you come to us, inhaling our news:
the tribunals open for you,

the laundries shake their gleaming linen.
Software tracks
your keystrokes, your fingertips,

the clouds move in their databases
and just like old times
money swings its golden fists.

Here on the table
brandy, cigars, the lamp
lighting your way

to your own words.
Climb somehow over, somehow
enter: from falling ash,

from brandy vapour,
from the muttered ghosts of poems
I'd sneak the watchfulness

that lets nothing go,
plunder the rage and the caress
in the world-stung trek to the desk.

Out the window, for belief,
another tree, the scrawny plum tree
no one will ever credit

since no one's seen a plum. And yet —
And yet it is a plum tree,
you can tell it by the leaf.

Acknowledgements and Notes

Acknowledgements are due to the following where some of these poems or versions of them first appeared: *2012: Twenty Irish Poets Respond to Science* (Dedalus), *Akzente, Cyphers, Dekadentzya, The Irish Times, Manchester Review, Poetry International, Poetry Ireland Review, RTE, Shine On* (Dedalus) and *The Stony Thursday Book*.

pp 76-100 Poems beginning with small capitals are relations, close, distant and otherwise, of poems by Bertolt Brecht. In some cases the versions are of individual stanzas or sections. Other poems contain versions of lines by Brecht, and others are invented. All are dedicated to the spirit of BB.